FLOWER◦FAIRIES
OF◦THE◦SPRING

Designed by Malcolm Smythe

Colour retouched by Elsa Godfrey

Copyright © 1985 The Estate of Cicely Mary Barker

This edition first published in hardback 1985,
and in paperback 1987 by
Blackie and Son Limited
7 Leicester Place, London WC2H 7BP

British Library Cataloguing in Publication Data
Barker, Cicely Mary
    Flower fairies of the spring. ——(The flower fairies)
    I. Title   II. Series
    821'.912   PR6003.A6786
    ISBN 0-216-91688-7
    ISBN 0-216-92148-1 Pbk

Printed in Great Britain by Cambus Litho, East Kilbride

FLOWER·FAIRIES
OF·THE·SPRING

Poems and pictures by
CICELY MARY BARKER

BLACKIE

THE SONG OF THE
CROCUS FAIRY

Crocus of yellow, new and gay;
Mauve and purple, in brave array;
    Crocus white
    Like a cup of light, –
Hundreds of them are smiling up,
Each with a flame in its shining cup,
By the touch of the warm and welcome sun
Opened suddenly. Spring's begun!
Dance then, fairies, for joy, and sing
The song of the coming again of Spring.

CROCUS

THE SONG OF THE
HAZEL CATKIN FAIRY

Like little tails of little lambs,
  On leafless twigs my catkins swing;
They dingle-dangle merrily
  Before the wakening of Spring.

Beside the pollen-laden tails
  My tiny crimson tufts you see,
The promise of the autumn nuts
  Upon the slender hazel tree.

While yet the woods lie grey and still
  I give my tidings: "Spring is near!"
One day the land shall leap to life
  With fairies calling: "Spring is *here*!"

HAZEL CATKIN

THE SONG OF THE
COLTSFOOT FAIRY

The winds of March are keen and cold;
I fear them not, for I am bold.

I wait not for my leaves to grow;
They follow after: they are slow.

My yellow blooms are brave and bright;
I greet the Spring with all my might.

COLTSFOOT

THE SONG OF THE
CELANDINE FAIRY

Before the hawthorn leaves unfold,
Or buttercups put forth their gold,
By every sunny footpath shine
The stars of Lesser Celandine.

CELANDINE

THE SONG OF THE
WILLOW CATKIN FAIRY

The people call me Palm, they do;
They call me Pussy-Willow too.
And when I'm in full bloom, the bees
Come humming round my yellow trees.

The people trample round about
And spoil the little trees, and shout;
My shiny twigs are thin and brown:
The people pull and break them down.

To keep a Holy Feast, they say,
They take my pretty boughs away.
I should be glad – I should not mind –
If only people weren't unkind.

Oh, you may pick a piece, you may
(So dear and silky, soft and grey);
But if you're rough and greedy, why
You'll make the little fairies cry.

WILLOW CATKIN

THE SONG OF THE
WINDFLOWER FAIRY

While human-folk slumber,
    The fairies espy
Stars without number.
    Sprinkling the sky.

The Winter's long sleeping,
    Like night-time, is done;
But day-stars are leaping
    To welcome the sun.

Star-like they sprinkle
    The wildwood with light;
Countless they twinkle –
    The Windflowers white!

WINDFLOWER

THE SONG OF THE
DAISY FAIRY

Come to me and play with me,
  I'm the babies' flower;
Make a necklace gay with me,
Spend the whole long day with me,
  Till the sunset hour.

I must say Good-night, you know,
  Till tomorrow's playtime;
Close my petals tight, you know,
Shut the red and white, you know,
  Sleeping till the daytime.

DAISY

THE SONG OF THE
DANDELION FAIRY

Here's the Dandelion's rhyme:
    See my leaves with tooth-like edges;
Blow my clocks to tell the time;
    See me flaunting by the hedges,
In the meadow, in the lane,
    Gay and naughty in the garden;
Pull me up – I grow again,
    Asking neither leave nor pardon.
Sillies, what are you about
    With your spades and hoes of iron?
You can never drive me out –
    Me, the dauntless Dandelion!

DANDELION

THE SONG OF THE
DAFFODIL FAIRY

I'm everyone's darling: the blackbird and
    starling
Are shouting about me from blossoming
    boughs;
For I, the Lent Lily, the Daffy-down-dilly,
Have heard through the country the call to
    arouse.
The orchards are ringing with voices
    a-singing
The praise of my petticoat, praise of my
    gown;
The children are playing, and hark! they are
    saying
That Daffy-down-dilly is come up to town!

DAFFODIL

THE SONG OF THE
DOG VIOLET FAIRY

The wren and robin hop around;
    The Primrose-maids my neighbours be;
The sun has warmed the mossy ground;
Where Spring has come, I too am found:
    The Cuckoo's call has wakened me!

DOG VIOLET

THE SONG OF THE
PRIMROSE FAIRY

The Primrose opens wide in spring;
    Her scent is sweet and good:
It smells of every happy thing
    In sunny lane and wood.
I have not half the skill to sing
    And praise her as I should.

She's dear to folk throughout the land;
    In her is nothing mean:
She freely spreads on every hand
    Her petals pale and clean.
And though she's neither proud nor grand,
    She is the Country Queen.

PRIMROSE

THE SONG OF THE
LADY'S SMOCK FAIRY

Where the grass is damp and green,
Where the shallow streams are flowing,
Where the cowslip buds are showing,
   I am seen.

Dainty as a fairy's frock,
White or mauve, of elfin sewing,
'Tis the meadow-maiden growing –
   Lady's Smock.

LADY'S SMOCK

THE SONG OF THE
LARCH FAIRY

Sing a song of Larch trees
    Loved by fairy-folk;
Dark stands the pinewood,
    Bare stands the oak,
But the Larch is dressed and trimmed
    Fit for fairy-folk!

Sing a song of Larch trees,
    Sprays that swing aloft,
Pink tufts, and tassels
    Grass-green and soft:
All to please the little elves
    Singing songs aloft!

LARCH

THE SONG OF THE
BLUEBELL FAIRY

My hundred thousand bells of blue,
　　The splendour of the Spring,
They carpet all the woods anew
With royalty of sapphire hue;
The Primrose is the Queen, 'tis true.
　　But surely I am King!
　　　　Ah yes,
　　The peerless Woodland King!

Loud, loud the thrushes sing their song;
　　The bluebell woods are wide;
My stems are tall and straight and strong;
From ugly streets the children throng,
They gather armfuls, great and long,
　　Then home they troop in pride –
　　　　Ah yes,
　　With laughter and with pride!

BLUEBELL

THE SONG OF THE
STITCHWORT FAIRY

I am brittle-stemmed and slender,
But the grass is my defender.

On the banks where grass is long,
I can stand erect and strong.

All my mass of starry faces
Looking up from wayside places,

From the thick and tangled grass,
Gives you greeting as you pass.

STITCHWORT

THE SONG OF THE
SPEEDWELL FAIRY

Clear blue are the skies;
   My petals are blue;
   As beautiful, too,
As bluest of eyes.

The heavens are high:
   By the field-path I grow
   Where wayfarers go,
And "Good speed" say I;

"See, here is a prize
   Of wonderful worth:
   A weed of the earth,
As blue as the skies!"

SPEEDWELL

THE SONG OF THE
COWSLIP FAIRY

The land is full of happy birds
And flocks of sheep and grazing herds.

I hear the songs of larks that fly
Above me in the breezy sky.

I hear the little lambkins bleat;
My honey-scent is rich and sweet.

Beneath the sun I dance and play
In April and in merry May.

The grass is green as green can be;
The children shout at sight of me.

COWSLIP

THE SONG OF THE
HEART'S-EASE FAIRY

Like the richest velvet
    (I've heard the fairies tell)
Grow the handsome pansies
    Within the garden wall;
When you praise their beauty,
    Remember me as well –
Think of little Heart's-ease,
    The brother of them all!

Come away and seek me
    When the year is young,
Through the open ploughlands
    Beyond the garden wall;
Many names are pretty
    And many songs are sung;
Mine – because I'm Heart's-ease –
    Are prettiest of all!

HEART'S-EASE

THE SONG OF THE
MAY FAIRY

My buds, they cluster small and green;
    The sunshine gaineth heat:
Soon shall the hawthorn tree be clothed
    As with a snowy sheet.

O magic sight, the hedge is white,
    My scent is very sweet;
And lo, where I am come indeed,
    The Spring and Summer meet.

MAY